Wilbur and Orville Wright

THE FLIGHT TO ADVENTURE

Wilbur and Orville Wright

THE FLIGHT TO ADVENTURE

by Louis Sabin
illustrated by John Lawn

Troll Associates

Library of Congress Cataloging in Publication Data

Sabin, Louis.
   Wilbur and Orville Wright, the flight to adventure.

   Summary: Focuses on the childhood of the Wright
brothers and the inventiveness they displayed from
their earliest days.
    1. Wright, Wilbur, 1867-1912—Juvenile literature.
2. Wright Orville, 1871-1948—Juvenile literature.
[1. Wright, Wilbur, 1867-1912. 2. Wright, Orville,
1871-1948. 3. Aeronautics—Biography] 1. Lawn,
John, ill. II. Title.
TL540.W7S24 1983   629.13'0092'2 [B] [920]   82-15879
ISBN 0-89375-851-5
ISBN 0-89375-852-3 (pbk.)

Wilbur and Orville Wright

THE FLIGHT TO ADVENTURE

August 19, 1871 was a sunny, steamy day in
Dayton, Ohio. The three Wright brothers
sprawled under a tall tree in front of the white
frame house at 7 Hawthorn Street. It was too
hot to play ball or tag, too hot to do much of
anything. Besides, something important was
happening in the house, and the boys wanted to
stay nearby.

7

The screen door swung open, and Milton Wright stepped out onto the wide front porch. "You can come in now, boys," he said, smiling. "There's a fine baby brother waiting to meet you."

Ten-year-old Reuchlin, eight-year-old Lorin, and four-year-old Wilbur Wright rushed up the porch steps into the house. Without stopping, they dashed upstairs to the second floor and into their parents' bedroom.

Their mother, Susan Wright, was sitting up in bed, holding the newborn baby. "Children," she said, "I'd like you to meet Orville." Then, smiling at the baby in her arms, she added, "Orville, here are your three big brothers."

The baby yawned and closed his eyes. The three boys, standing next to the bed, laughed loudly. Wilbur moved closer. "When will he be big enough to play with me?" he asked. "Reuchlin and Lorin have each other, so Orville has to be *my* best friend."

Mr. Wright picked up Wilbur and hugged him. "Soon enough, son," he told the four-year-old. "And I know you two will be best friends. Just give Orville a little time to grow."

Wilbur and Orville were very close right from the start, and they stayed that way all through their lives. As Wilbur wrote many years later, "From the time we were little children, my brother Orville and I lived together, played together, worked together, and in fact, thought together. We usually owned all of our toys in common. We talked over our thoughts . . . and nearly everything that was done in our lives has been the result of discussions between us."

When Orville was five years old, he was given a special kind of toy called a gyroscopic top. It had two wheels, one inside the other. The outside wheel would spin up and down, while the inside wheel would spin from side to side. The top had such perfect balance that it could keep spinning even when it was set on the edge of a knife blade.

Orville and Wilbur played with the new toy for hours. Like all mechanical things, it fascinated the brothers. They wanted to know how the top worked. So Wilbur, who was a very good reader, went to the library. He came home with as many books as he could find about tops and gyroscopes. Then he read the books to Orville, and they talked about them. Much of the science was too hard for the boys to understand, but they did learn some things.

Many times, when the boys had a question about mechanical things, they asked their mother. Susan Wright was an unusual woman for the nineteenth century. In those days, not many men and even fewer women had much education. But Mrs. Wright, like her husband, was a college graduate. She was especially good at mathematics and science and anything mechanical. When something around the house had to be fixed, Mrs. Wright did the job. If she wanted to make or fix something, but did not have the tool to do it, she made the tool herself.

Once, when she couldn't find a sled big enough for Orville and Wilbur to ride on together, she solved the problem by building one out of spare wood and metal parts from an old stove.

Mrs. Wright helped the boys learn how the gyroscopic top worked. Most of the time, though, she wanted them to figure things out by themselves. Mr. Wright agreed that the boys should learn as much as they could on their own. Often, when the children asked him for some information, he would say, "Look it up in a book. If I tell you the answer, you'll probably forget it. But if you find it yourself, you'll remember it a great deal longer. Best of all, you'll know where to find it again if you *do* forget. That's what books are for."

There were plenty of books right in the house. In the living room, where the family spent hours every evening, there were bookcases filled with novels, fairy tales, biographies of famous men and women, history books, dictionaries, and two full sets of encyclopedias. In those days, long before the invention of radio, television, and the movies, reading was a main form of entertainment. Many evenings in the Wright home were spent listening to one of the family members read aloud from a book, newspaper, or magazine.

The Wrights also believed that their children should learn to be independent, so every one of the young Wrights earned spending money by doing odd jobs. Orville and Wilbur were paid one penny each night for washing and drying the dinner dishes. All of the children were paid for running errands, cleaning out the fireplaces, shoveling snow, chopping firewood—any useful job that needed to be done.

In 1878, when Wilbur was eleven and Orville was almost seven, the family moved to Cedar Rapids, Iowa. Mr. Wright, who was a bishop in the United Brethren Church, had been given a parish in that city. Here, in their new home on Adams Street, the boys were given a gift that would one day help them change the history of the world.

Mr. Wright brought a gift with him when he came home from a business trip. It was a small "flying machine" that flew like a helicopter. It was made of cork, bamboo, and thin paper. The machine's "motor" was a rubber band that had to be twisted many times. When the rubber band couldn't be twisted any more, the person holding the machine let go. It rose straight up, hovered for a few seconds above everybody's heads, then floated down to the floor.

The boys nicknamed their flying toy the Bat. They played with it day and night until, finally, the paper tore and the rubber band snapped. Instead of trying to repair the toy, they decided to build a new, improved Bat. Orville was still too young to do much of the work on it, but he helped Wilbur whenever he could.

Their first homemade model was a little bit bigger than the original flying machine. It was roughly made and didn't fly very well.

"Why won't it fly?" Orville asked his brother.

"Maybe we cut the bamboo pieces too thick," Wilbur said. "Besides, we didn't do a very careful job. It's really kind of messy."

"Could we make another one? I've saved up ten cents. We can use it to buy the rubber bands," Orville said.

"Okay, Orville. I have twenty-five cents," Wilbur said. "That will be enough for the rest of the stuff we need. But this time let's make a really big Bat—and fly it outside!"

The boys bought the material they needed and drew the plans. For weeks they worked on their flying machine. Every day after school, they rushed home, did their homework, and continued to build the Big Bat. At last, it was ready for its first flight.

One bright Saturday morning, Orville and Wilbur called the family outside to see the Big Bat fly. They set up chairs on the porch for their mother and father. Reuchlin, Lorin, and their four-year-old sister, Katherine, sat on the porch steps.

Orville held the Bat while Wilbur twisted the double-thick rubber band. "Ready," Wilbur said. "When I count to three, let it fly. One . . . two . . . three!"

Orville let go. For a second, the Bat hung in the air, then it crashed to the ground. Both boys turned sad faces to their family. There was a moment's silence, then Orville wailed, "Thirty-five cents! Think of all the ice cream we could have had."

The family burst into laughter. After a few seconds, Mrs. Wright said, "It almost flew. Why don't you boys try again?"

"Not right now, Mother," Wilbur said. "We don't know enough about making a flying machine. Anyway, Orville and I don't have any more money."

When the brothers weren't working on one kind of machine or another, they did the things most boys did in those days. They went to the local public schools. They played baseball in the spring and summer, and football in the fall.

In the winter, they ice-skated and played hockey at the local pond. They also swam there in the summer.

But much of the brothers' outside playtime wasn't spent together. Wilbur was in junior high, and his friends were eleven and twelve years old. They didn't want to have anything to do with Orville and his grade-school friends. At home, however, the brothers were still as close as ever.

In 1881, when Orville was ten and Wilbur was fourteen, the Wrights moved again. This time, it was to Richmond, Indiana. That summer Orville found a new hobby that took up all of his time: making and flying kites. He even sold some to other youngsters. Everyone agreed that Orville was a great kite-maker.

Orville earned spending money in other ways. He delivered newspapers once a week for a local church. He also took his wagon around the neighborhood every day after school. One of his daily trips was to a chain factory where he picked up pieces of scrap metal. Orville also collected anything people threw away that he thought he could sell. Then, on Saturday, he brought his week's collection to a local junk yard. He never made more than a few cents at a time, but this never discouraged him.

Orville had a reason for earning this money. He wanted to buy the parts to build a lathe, a machine that holds a piece of metal or wood while it is being turned and shaped by a worker. Finally, Orville had enough money, but the lathe he made was too small to be very useful. This disappointed him.

Wilbur came to the rescue. He offered to help Orville build a really big lathe. Once it was done, they could do all kinds of woodworking jobs, like putting up a fancy, new front porch. Orville loved the idea, and they set to work making the lathe right away.

The lathe was built in the barn behind the Wright house. It was powered by foot pedals like the ones on a bicycle. It worked perfectly. By the spring of 1882, the Wright house had a spanking new front porch, complete with handsome railings and posts. Every inch of it had been made by the two young Wright brothers. Soon they were earning money by making wooden things for people in the neighborhood.

Wilbur was pleased with their success, but he had a new idea. The lathe rattled and needed to be oiled all the time. Wilbur had noticed that bicycles used ball bearings to make them run smoothly. Why not put ball bearings on the lathe for the same reason? He decided to give it a try.

Behind the barn, Wilbur found a couple of metal rings that had been part of the harness for a horse. He didn't have steel ball bearings—they cost too much—so he used clay marbles instead. When the marbles were fitted into the rings, Wilbur attached his invention to the lathe.

All of the youngsters in the neighborhood came to see the Wright brothers' latest contraption in action. Orville sat down and began to pedal. Wilbur had a fresh piece of wood ready for shaping. Suddenly, there was a loud noise. *Rattle-bang-crash!* The whole barn shook.

"Gol-ly!" gasped one of the boys. "A couple more turns of your ball bearings and this whole barn will fall apart. Looks like you made a mistake this time, Wilbur."

Wilbur checked his new invention and saw that it really didn't work very well. The pedaling had crushed the clay marbles. *But why did that make the whole barn shake?* he wondered. It was a mystery that was solved a few minutes later. The boys found out that a cyclone had passed through Richmond at the same time Orville began to pedal!

The next brilliant Wright idea was Orville's. It came to him while playing with Gansey Johnston, the boy who lived in the house next door. Gansey's father had an interesting hobby —stuffing dead animals. The Johnston's barn was filled with a giant grizzly bear, a black bear, several ducks, a raccoon, a beaver, and a number of other animals. Every one looked almost alive.

"Do you know what, Gansey?" Orville said. "We could have a circus, using all of these animals. We could hold it right here in the barn. I know a couple of boys who can tumble and juggle, and Wilbur has a friend who rides a unicycle. We can make some money by charging admission. Do you want to be my partner?"

Gansey agreed that it was a terrific scheme. So did Harry Morrow, who wanted to get into the partnership. So the Great W. J. & M. Circus was born. Plans were immediately made to stage a parade and a number of acts in the barn. That night, Orville told Wilbur about the great circus.

"Don't you think it's going to be wonderful?" Orville said. "We're going to charge three cents for kids under three years old and five cents for everybody else. I bet we'll make a lot of money."

Wilbur thought for a moment. Then, half-joking, he said that such a grand show deserved a notice in a local newspaper, the Richmond *Evening Item*. He offered to write a description of the "circus" and give it to the paper. Orville and his partners loved the idea.

Wilbur's article, which was printed, used words such as *mammoth, stupendous,* and *colossal*. It attracted so many people to the "circus" that there wasn't enough room to hold them all.

Some of the people who paid admission were annoyed to find that it wasn't a real circus. But most just laughed and said that anyone with such a good imagination was sure to be a success. They willingly paid the few pennies to look at the stuffed animals and watch the young performers.

When school let out in June 1884, the Wright family moved back to Dayton, Ohio. This would be their home from then on. In September, when school began again, Orville went into seventh grade—but not before facing a problem. It wasn't that he was a poor student. In fact, he was very good in school. But he had been up to some mischief at the Richmond school the past June. His teacher had sent him home and told him not to come back without his parents. Only the Wrights moved before they could get to see the teacher.

So, in September, Orville arrived at the
Dayton school without proof that he had
finished sixth grade. At first, the school
principal didn't want to let him into seventh
grade. Orville explained what had happened in
Richmond. He swore he would behave himself.
He promised to work hard in all of his classes, if
they'd only give him a chance. At last, the
principal agreed. He wasn't sorry. Not only was
Orville an excellent student, he also finished the
year with the highest arithmetic mark in the
whole city of Dayton.

The move affected Wilbur's school record in a
different way. He didn't have any problems at
the Richmond high school. It was simply that
the family move took place a few days before

graduation. If Wilbur wanted his official high-school diploma, he had to come back for graduation.

Wilbur felt that the piece of paper wasn't worth the trip back to Richmond. His parents said the decision was up to him. Mr. Wright added, "You went to school to learn. A diploma just tells others that you helped fill the class-rooms—not that anything of value filled your head."

Finishing high school—even without a diploma—did not end Wilbur's education. Of all the Wright children, Wilbur was the one who most loved books. He was always teaching him-self new subjects from library books. He also took advanced courses in Greek and math-ematics at Dayton Central High School. He even planned to go away to college, until he had a bad accident. The winter before he was to leave, he took a bad fall in an ice-hockey game. The doctor advised him to take it easy and let time heal his injuries.

Both boys continued to work with mechanical things. Orville and his friend, Ed Sines, set up their own printing company. They used a small printing press to put out a newspaper, called *The Midget*, which they sold to their classmates. The partners had a lot of fun doing it, but they didn't make any money at it. So Wilbur suggested that Orville and Ed take on small printing jobs for Dayton businessmen.

The boys took his suggestion, and they did very nicely with their printing work. They were even able to hire a classmate to help them—for a salary of fifteen cents a week. Most of the time, their customers paid in cash. A few didn't pay at all. And one, who owed them two dollars, offered to pay them in popping corn. They took the corn to a grocer, who gave them two dollars for it. Orville wanted to invest the money in more printing equipment, but Ed didn't.

"As hard as we work and as much money as we make, I never have any to spend," Ed complained. "I wish we'd popped the corn for ourselves. I'm tired of working for nothing. Why don't we figure out how much the business is worth. Then you give me half, and the business is all yours."

Orville liked this idea. He borrowed money from Wilbur to pay Ed his half of what the business was worth. Now Orville had a new partner—Wilbur. Together, they made the printing press better and larger.

With the same kind of inventiveness that their mother had shown, the boys put together a superb press. They collected pieces of wood from the Wright barn, pieces of metal from a junk yard, and parts of the old family buggy. Wilbur drew careful plans for the new printing press. The plans didn't seem to follow the rules

of mechanics, and everyone was sure that the press wouldn't work. But it did, and very well!

One day, a finely dressed man walked into the Wright brothers' printing shop and asked to see the homemade press. He explained that he was in the printing business in another town and had heard about Wilbur's invention. He looked the machine over from top to bottom, inside and out. He even lay down on the floor, under the machine, to watch it run from that angle. Finally, he said, "It works all right. But I still don't understand *why* it works."

While Orville went to high school during the day, Wilbur ran the printing business. They worked together after school and on weekends, putting out the *West Side News*, a weekly newspaper. They also did printing jobs for local businesses. Ed Sines worked for them. He was a reporter and advertising salesman for the paper.

When Orville finished high school in 1890, he went to work with Wilbur full time. Soon business was so good that the Wright brothers hired a new reporter. He was Paul Laurence Dunbar, who would one day be a well-known poet. On the wall of the shop, the young Dunbar wrote these words:

> *Orville Wright is out of sight*
> *In the printing business.*
> *No other mind is half so bright*
> *As his'n is.*

In 1892, Orville and Wilbur got involved in a new hobby—bicycles. Orville even became a bicycle racer for a while. Within a few months, this hobby became another Wright brothers' business. They made Ed Sines manager of the printing shop, which left them free to sell and repair bicycles. They also custom-made bicycles and had three models: the Van Cleve, the St. Clair, and the Wright Special.

As much as they enjoyed their successful business, the Wright brothers never stopped thinking about flying machines. They read everything they could about ballooning, about gliding, and about different kinds of flying machines that had been tried through the years. They wrote to people all over the world who shared their dream of flying.

At the same time, Orville and Wilbur began to work on their own designs for a real flying machine. They used every idea they had ever

learned from childhood on—from their
experiments with the Big Bat, with kite
building, and from the experience of making
their own printing presses, lathes, and bicycles.

In 1899, the Wright brothers flew their first gliders. These were large, double-winged kites. After testing more than 1,000 gliders, the brothers were ready to try a flying machine powered by an engine.

In the fall of 1903, Orville and Wilbur were unsuccessful due to bad weather and mechanical troubles. Finally, the brothers succeeded. On December 17, 1903, at 10:35 in the morning at Kitty Hawk, North Carolina, their power-driven, heavier-than-air machine took off and flew! It stayed in the air twelve full seconds, traveled about one hundred-twenty feet, and flew at the speed of over seven miles per hour. The Wright brothers had opened the door to the Age of Flight!

Orville and Wilbur continued to improve their original airplane. And they were always their own test pilots. There was a setback every now and then, but that didn't stop them. They kept right on going—higher and farther each year.

After Wilbur died, on May 30, 1912, Orville kept on designing better flying machines. It was a devotion to aviation that ended only with his death, on January 30, 1948.

The Wright brothers turned the dream of flying into a reality. Today, as we reach farther and farther into space, the world owes a huge debt to the vision and creativity of Wilbur and Orville Wright.